m

INTERIM SITE WITH

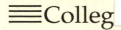

≡Colleg

College SURVIVAL Cookbook

Nadine Z. Ujevich

Illustrated by Karla Shaffer

ISBN 0-8229-5491-5
Copyright © 1989, 1991, 1992 Nadine Z. Ujevich
All rights reserved
Manufactured in Canada
Designed and typeset in the United States of America
Printed on acid-free paper

Distributed by the University of Pittsburgh Press
c/o CUP Services
Box 6525
Ithaca, NY 14851
Phone: 800-666-2211

Eurospan, London

To my niece,
VALERIE ZERNICH,
a college coed.

Thank you
RENEE, MARK, JAN, GARY, AND TOM,
whose help made this book possible.

CONTENTS

INTRODUCTION

COLLEGE AND UNIVERSITY STUDENTS love to eat. Once at school most students can no longer enjoy the convenience of living at home with good old-fashioned home-cooked meals. With limited knowledge and experience in cooking, they attempt to squeeze in the everyday kitchen duty along with their additional responsibilities of study and other school activities.

In most instances the kitchen facilities and cookware in dormitories and apartments are limited. Many students will, therefore, neglect to prepare meals and settle for a diet of "junk food."

It was apparent to me that a compact guide for cooking had to be composed with an easy-to-follow format that would provide a variety of wholesome nutritious meals which were moderately priced. Consideration had to be given to the unavailability of cookware. I wrote this cookbook to fulfill this need.

Included you will find a variety of simple-to-prepare breakfasts, lunches, dinners, snacks, and party treats. There are also lists of helpful timesaving tips and suggestions for purchasing basic cookware and supplies along with a simple to use weights and measures chart.

The large variety of over 150 recipes should adequately satisfy most appetites.

This cookbook undoubtedly will remain useful long after the college days are over.

Appetizers, Beverages & Party Drinks

WING DINGS

Frozen breaded chicken wings are available at your food market.

INGREDIENTS

12 frozen wing dings or lightly floured fresh wings
¼ cup shortening or oil
salt (*optional*)

Heat shortening in skillet on medium-high heat. You may check to see if shortening is at proper cooking temperature by dropping a bread crumb into the hot shortening. If it sizzles, oil is ready for frying. Add six wings at a time to the skillet. If you don't overcrowd the skillet, the wings will brown quicker. Fry wings, turning to brown both sides. Remove from skillet and place wings on absorbent paper to remove excess grease. Add salt if desired.

SALMON BALL

INGREDIENTS

1 (16 oz.) can salmon, drained and flaked
1 tablespoon onion, finely chopped
1 tablespoon lemon juice
½ teaspoon salt
¼ teaspoon liquid smoke
8 ounces cream cheese, softened
⅓ cup parsley flakes

In bowl, combine and mix by hand all ingredients except parsley flakes. Cover and refrigerate until cool (approximately three hours). When cool, form into a ball and roll in parsley flakes. Cover and refrigerate until ready to serve. Garnish with apple wedges that have been dipped in lemon juice. Serve with crackers.

CHEESY STUFFED MUSHROOMS

A
P
P
E
T
I
Z
E
R
S

INGREDIENTS

1 pound fresh mushrooms
¼ cup butter
½ teaspoon salt
¼ teaspoon pepper
¼ cup grated cheese (mozzarella,
blue cheese, or other choice)
2 tablespoons bread crumbs
1 tablespoon lemon juice

Wash mushrooms in cold water. Separate stems and buttons of mushrooms. Chop stems. In skillet, sauté chopped stems in butter. Add salt and pepper to taste. Add cheese and bread crumbs. Stir. Remove mixture from heat and stuff mushroom caps. Sprinkle tops with lemon juice. Place stuffed mushrooms on a baking dish and bake 10 to 15 minutes at 350°.

SALAMI-CHEESE STACKS

INGREDIENTS

12 slices salami
11 slices cheese (American, provolone, or Cheddar)
8 olives

Stack, alternating salami and cheese until all slices are used. Cut stack into 8 pie-shaped wedges. Place a toothpick through each wedge to hold layers together. Separate the stacked layered wedges and add an olive to each toothpick.

INSTANT PIZZA

INGREDIENTS

6 English muffins
1 (4 oz.) can tomato sauce
12 thin slices mozzarella cheese
48 thin slices pepperoni
½ cup Parmesan cheese, grated
1 teaspoon oregano

Slice muffins in half. Spread tomato sauce on each half. Sprinkle with Parmesan cheese and oregano. Place four slices pepperoni on each. Top with mozzarella cheese. Place on cookie sheet or aluminum foil and bake at 350° until cheese bubbles, approximately 10 minutes.

FRIED ONION RINGS

INGREDIENTS

½ cup shortening or oil
¾ teaspoon salt
1 tablespoon cornstarch
1 tablespoon oil
1 cup milk
¾ to 1 cup flour
2 to 3 large onions peeled,
sliced crossways, and separated into rings

Preheat shortening in frying pan. In bowl, combine and blend salt, cornstarch, and 1 tablespoon oil. Gradually add milk. Stir in flour until batter is the consistency of thin pancake batter. Beat until smooth. Dip onion rings in batter a few at a time, and place them into the hot grease. Do not crowd the pan. Cook the rings until they are puffy and golden brown. Place on paper towels to absorb excess grease.

MINIATURE REUBEN

(6 sandwiches)

INGREDIENTS

1 package small party rye bread, 12 slices bread
6 slices corned beef
½ cup Russian dressing
1 cup sauerkraut, well drained
3 slices Swiss cheese, cut in halves

Spread Russian dressing on slice of rye bread. Add sliced corned beef, kraut, and a slice of cheese. Top with second slice of bread. Bake on a baking tray or aluminum foil at 350° until cheese melts.

INGREDIENTS

6 eggs (hard-boiled)
½ cup mayonnaise
1 teaspoon vinegar
1 teaspoon dry mustard
½ teaspoon salt
dash of pepper
3 or 4 olives with pimento

Remove shells from hard-boiled eggs. Cut eggs in half lengthwise. Remove yolks and place them in a small bowl. Combine yolks with mayonnaise, vinegar, dry mustard, salt, and pepper. Mix. Fill egg whites with yolk mixture. Lightly sprinkle paprika over yolk filling. Slice olives. Place one slice on top of each filled egg.

**A
P
P
E
T
I
Z
E
R
S**

INGREDIENTS

1 bag tortilla or corn chips
½ pound Cheddar cheese
Small jar of green chili peppers or
jalapeño peppers (*optional*)

Preheat oven to 400°. Place tortilla chips in a single layer on a baking sheet or aluminum foil. Cut cheese slices in quarters and place one piece on top of each chip. Top with chili or jalapeño peppers. Bake until cheese melts.

LAYERED TACO-AVOCADO DIP

INGREDIENTS

1 (16 oz.) can refried beans
1 jar picante sauce, medium/hot
2 ripe avocados, mashed
½ cup mayonnaise
1 cup (8 oz.) sour cream
1 package taco seasoning
1 tomato, chopped
shredded lettuce
2 cups Cheddar cheese, shredded
½ can pitted black olives, chopped

Spread refried beans on bottoms of two 9-inch pie pans. Add picante sauce, spreading it over the beans. In a separate bowl, mash avocados and add mayonnaise. Mix well. Spread this over the picante layer. In separate small bowl, combine sour cream and taco seasoning, mix well by hand, and spread over the avocado-mayonnaise layer. Place a layer of chopped tomatoes on next. Last three layers are: shredded lettuce, shredded cheese, and black olives. Cover and refrigerate overnight. Serve with tortilla chips.

INGREDIENTS

2 large potatoes
4 tablespoons melted butter
1 teaspoon salt
½ teaspoon pepper
¼ teaspoon onion and garlic salt (*optional*)
½ cup shredded sharp Cheddar cheese,
grated Parmesan cheese, or peanut butter

Preheat oven to 400°. Wash potatoes and wrap individually in aluminum foil. Pierce potatoes through foil with a fork and bake in hot oven until soft (about 1½ hours). Remove potatoes from oven and scoop out almost all of the potato, leaving a small amount adhering to the potato skins. Cut skins into strips, about 3" by 1". Coat each strip completely with melted butter and season. Bake on ungreased cookie sheet or aluminum foil for 10 to 15 minutes until crisp. Top with cheese or peanut butter and return to oven and melt.

───────── CELERY SNACKS ─────────

INGREDIENTS

4 celery stalks
¼ cup peanut butter or 3 ounces cream cheese
¼ teaspoon paprika (*optional*)

Wash celery stalks. Fill concave part of celery with peanut butter or cream cheese. Cut celery into finger-sized pieces. Sprinkle cheese lightly with paprika.

FANCY FROSTED GRAPES

INGREDIENTS

2 pounds seedless green grapes
1 egg white
1 (3 oz.) package gelatin, any flavor

Beat egg white in bowl. Dip small bunches of grapes in egg white, allowing excess to drain off. Sprinkle with gelatin. Chill in refrigerator overnight or for several hours. Use as a garnish.

*Quiche can be prepared ahead,
chilled, and baked a half hour before serving.*

INGREDIENTS

1 frozen pie shell
3 slices provolone cheese
3 tablespoons dehydrated onion soup mix
½ cup grated Swiss cheese
3 eggs
1 egg yolk
2 cups light cream
¼ teaspoon salt
¼ teaspoon pepper
1 tablespoon butter

Bake a pie shell at 400° for 5 minutes. Remove from oven and cool. Place provolone cheese slices on bottom of pie shell. Combine onion soup mix and Swiss cheese and sprinkle over provolone. In bowl, beat eggs, egg yolk, light cream, salt, and pepper. Pour over onion soup mix. Heat butter, slightly browning it, and pour over top. Bake at 375° approximately 30 to 35 minutes until solid. Remove from oven and cool before serving.

QUICHE LORRAINE

INGREDIENTS

1 frozen pie shell
½ pound bacon, fried crisp, drained, and crumbled
½ pound Swiss or Gruyère cheese, shredded
4 eggs, beaten
1 tablespoon flour
½ teaspoon salt
½ teaspoon celery salt
¼ teaspoon cayenne pepper
¼ teaspoon nutmeg
1½ cups light cream
1 onion, chopped
2 tablespoons butter

Bake pastry at 400° until lightly browned. Cool. Add crumbled bacon to crust, reserving 2 tablespoons for trim. Add cheese. Sauté onion by simmering in butter until soft. Combine and add remaining ingredients to the onions and pour over cheese. Sprinkle reserved bacon over top. Bake for 30 to 40 minutes at 375° until cooked through.

B
E
V
E
R
A
G
E
S

&

P
A
R
T
Y

D
R
I
N
K
S

CRANBERRY PUNCH

(25 servings)

INGREDIENTS

1 quart cranberry juice cocktail, cooled
1 (6 oz.) can of frozen pink lemonade, thawed
2 quarts ginger ale, cooled

Mix all in a large bowl and serve.

CRAN-RASPBERRY PUNCH

INGREDIENTS

28 ounces ginger ale
2 pints raspberry sherbet, softened
½ cup lemon juice
2 cups orange juice
½ cup sugar
48 ounces cranberry juice

Mix all of the above ingredients together except the
sherbet. Refrigerate. Add sherbet before serving.

───STRAWBERRY FRUIT PUNCH───

INGREDIENTS

2 quarts chilled ginger ale
½ cup water
1 (6 oz.) can frozen orange juice (concentrate), thawed
1 cup lemon juice
2 (10 oz.) packages frozen strawberries, thawed
ice cubes

Combine orange juice, lemon juice, water and strawberries and refrigerate until cold. When ready to serve, place ice cubes in bowl. Add ginger ale and fruit mixture, stir.

───────SHERBET PUNCH───────

INGREDIENTS

3 pints sherbet (any flavor)
3 quarts ginger ale

Cool ginger ale. Mix with sherbet and serve.

───────HOT COCOA DRINK───────

(good served after cold outings)

INGREDIENTS

1 quart chocolate milk
½ pint whipping cream, whipped
chocolate sprinkles

Heat chocolate milk. Pour in cups. Top with whipped cream and chocolate sprinkles.

Main Meals

FRIED CHICKEN

INGREDIENTS

1 chicken, cut up in serving pieces or any selected pieces
1 teaspoon salt
1 cup flour
1 cup shortening

Wash chicken pieces in cold water. Salt lightly. Place flour in paper or plastic baggie. Put salted chicken in the bag of flour and shake. When chicken pieces are coated with flour remove them from the bag. Heat shortening in skillet. Add floured chicken to hot grease. Fry slowly, turning to brown all sides. Lower the heat and simmer until chicken is well-cooked.

M
A
I
N

M
E
A
L
S

INGREDIENTS

2 whole boneless chicken breasts, cut in cubes
1 tablespoon cornstarch
1 tablespoon soy sauce
1 teaspoon sugar
1 teaspoon ground ginger
¼ teaspoon crushed pepper
1½ teaspoons salt
3 medium zucchini
1 (6 oz.) package frozen peapods
1 pound small mushrooms
½ cup oil

In bowl combine cornstarch, soy sauce, sugar, ginger, red pepper, and salt. Add chicken and coat. Cut zucchini into bite-sized pieces. In large pot, heat oil. Cook zucchini and mushrooms, stirring constantly. Add salt. Remove from oil and set aside. In remaining oil, cook chicken mixture until tender, about 10 minutes. Stir. Combine chicken and zucchini mixture and mix. Heat through and serve with cooked rice.

ROAST CHICKEN & POTATOES

INGREDIENTS

1 whole chicken
1 teaspoon salt
4 potatoes

Heat oven to 400°. Remove package containing chicken innards (usually found inside chicken). Wash chicken in cold water. Lightly salt whole chicken. Place chicken in roasting pan, breast side up, uncovered. Bake, browning breast side. Turn over and brown underside. It should take 1 to 1½ hours to cook chicken. Remove chicken from oven. For potatoes: peel, wash in cold water, and salt lightly. Place potatoes in roaster pan around chicken before roasting chicken. Turn potatoes over when undersides are brown. Potatoes are done when they are easily pierced with a fork.

BROILED SPLIT (½) CHICKEN

INGREDIENTS

2 chicken halves
4 potatoes *(optional)*
½ teaspoon salt

Set oven on broil. Wash chicken with cold water. Salt lightly. Put halves, breast side up, in shallow pan or on broiling pan and place under broiler. Brown breast side and turn over. Brown underside. It should take approximately 1 hour to cook.

Note 1: Chicken legs, breasts, etc., can also be broiled by browning them in this manner.

Note 2: Sliced potatoes may be cooked at the same time if placed in lower part of broiling pan when you begin to broil the chicken. The juices from the chicken will flavor the potatoes.

21

MEAT & CHEESE TACO

INGREDIENTS

6 taco shells
½ pound ground beef
1 small onion, chopped
½ teaspoon chili powder
¼ teaspoon salt
1 tomato
shredded lettuce
pinch garlic powder
½ cup Cheddar cheese, shredded
½ pint salsa, taco sauce, or sour cream

Heat taco shells in preheated 250° oven. Brown beef and onion in a skillet. Add garlic powder and salt. After meat is browned, drain fat. Add chili powder. Remove taco shells from oven. Stuff shells with beef, tomato, lettuce, and cheese. Top with salsa, taco sauce, or sour cream.

PLAIN MEATBALLS

INGREDIENTS

2 pounds ground beef
2 eggs
1 medium onion, chopped *(optional)*
½ teaspoon salt
¼ teaspoon pepper
½ cup bread crumbs *(optional)*
2 to 3 tablespoons oil

In bowl combine ground beef, eggs, salt, and pepper. If desired, onions and/or bread crumbs may be added. Mix well and roll into golf ball or smaller-sized balls. Fry in hot oil until brown. Turn heat down and cook through.

MAIN MEALS

INGREDIENTS

2 pounds ground beef
½ teaspoon parsley
½ teaspoon salt
¼ teaspoon pepper
½ teaspoon garlic powder
½ teaspoon Italian seasoning
2 eggs
Italian-seasoned bread crumbs
3 to 4 tablespoons oil

Combine and mix all of the above, adding just enough bread crumbs to hold all ingredients together firmly. Roll into small balls and fry in 3 to 4 tablespoons heated oil until brown. Turn heat down and simmer until meatballs are cooked through.

——MEATBALLS & POTATOES IN—— MUSHROOM SAUCE

INGREDIENTS

2 pounds ground beef
½ teaspoon salt
¼ teaspoon pepper
1 onion, chopped
2 eggs
2 potatoes, peeled and cubed
1 can cream of mushroom soup
1 can cold water or milk

Mix together ground beef, salt, pepper, chopped onion, and eggs. Roll meat into walnut-sized balls and place them in a roasting pan. Mix together mushroom soup and water. Pour over meatballs. Add potato cubes. Cover with a lid and bake at 350° for 1 hour. Add more water if sauce gets too thick.

——————FRIED BONGERS——————

(2 to 4 servings)

INGREDIENTS

1 pound ground beef
1 egg
1 small onion, chopped
1 teaspoon parsley flakes
⅓ teaspoon salt
¼ teaspoon pepper

Combine beef, egg, onion, parsley flakes, salt, and pepper in a bowl. Roll mixed meat into small loaves, the size of large meatballs. Place oil in frying pan and heat. Fry, turning so that loaves are browned all around. After browning, turn heat down and cook slowly until meat is well-done. Remove bongers from grease after cooked.

PORCUPINE BALLS

INGREDIENTS

2 pounds ground beef
2 eggs
1 onion, chopped
½ teaspoon salt
¼ teaspoon pepper
1 teaspoon parsley flakes
½ cup long grain rice
1 (15 oz.) can tomato sauce
1 (10 oz.) can tomato soup

In small pan, place rice in cold water and bring to a boil. Boil 3 to 4 minutes and drain. In bowl, combine beef, eggs, chopped onion, salt, pepper, parsley flakes, and rice. Mix well. Roll mixture into golf ball sized balls and place in a roasting pan. In bowl, combine tomato sauce and tomato soup and pour over meat balls. Cover with lid and bake 45 minutes to 1 hour at 350°. Add a little water if sauce gets too thick.

M
A
I
N

M
E
A
L
S

INGREDIENTS

1 pound ground beef
½ teaspoon chili powder
1 (8 oz.) can tomato sauce
1 (15 oz.) can kidney beans

Brown beef in a small skillet. Sprinkle chili powder over meat and mix. Add tomato sauce and simmer until hot. Add kidney beans and simmer 5 to 10 minutes until beans are hot. If chili gets too thick, add very small amount of water.

Note: If using chili for hot dogs, omit beans.

—BAKED STUFFED GREEN PEPPERS—

INGREDIENTS

1 pound ground beef
6 medium green peppers
½ cup cooked rice *(optional)*
1 teaspoon salt
½ teaspoon pepper
1 egg
1 small onion, chopped
1 teaspoon parsley flakes
1 (15 oz.) can tomato sauce
½ cup water

Cut around and remove top stem of each pepper, allowing enough of an opening for stuffing. Remove seeds and rinse. Combine all of the above ingredients except tomato sauce and water. Stuff peppers with meat mixture. Any excess meat stuffing can be rolled into additional balls. Place stuffed peppers in a baking dish or roasting pan. In a small bowl, mix tomato sauce and water. Pour it over the stuffed peppers. Place lid on roasting pan and bake for 1 hour at 350°.

MEAT LOAF

Ingredients

2 pounds ground beef
2 eggs
½ teaspoon salt
¼ teaspoon pepper
1 onion, chopped
1 tablespoon parsley flakes *(optional)*

Mix all ingredients in a bowl. Roll mixture into a loaf. Place into a dry roasting pan. Roast uncovered 45 minutes to 1 hour at 350°. Cover with lid when loaf is brown.

Variation: Add 1 can cream of mushroom soup and 1 can milk, ½ pound clean fresh mushrooms, or add 1 can tomato soup and 1 can water to meat loaf halfway through the roasting time if sauce is desired.

BEEF BRISKET BARBECUE

Ingredients

beef brisket (2 pounds or larger)
½ cup ketchup
¼ cup honey
¼ cup cider vinegar
½ cup onion, finely chopped
1 tablespoon Worcestershire sauce
1½ teaspoons liquid smoke
1 small bay leaf
¼ teaspoon black pepper

Salt meat and place in ungreased baking pan or roaster. Mix the remaining ingredients together and pour over meat. Cover and bake 3 hours at 325° or until tender. Stir and baste 3 times while baking. Slice meat diagonally, across grain.

—MARINATED FILET MIGNON ROAST—

INGREDIENTS

1 filet mignon roast
½ teaspoon salt
¼ teaspoon pepper
1 teaspoon garlic powder
5 to 6 dashes Worcestershire sauce
½ cup preferred wine
1 teaspoon chopped parsley
½ pound melted butter
1 green pepper, sliced
1 onion, sliced
1 pound mushrooms

Place filet in roasting pan. Add salt, pepper, garlic powder, Worcestershire sauce, wine, parsley, and butter. Cover with lid and refrigerate 6 hours or overnight. Remove from refrigerator and add green peppers and onion slices. Place roast uncovered in oven and bake approximately 1½ hours depending on how well-done you prefer the meat. Check by making a slit through center of the roast. Add small amount of warm water if sauce gets too thick. Add mushrooms about 10 minutes before removing roast from oven. Baste roast occasionally with its own sauce.

—BROILED STEAK—

INGREDIENTS

1 steak (e.g., filet mignon, strip steak, rib eye, sirloin, T-bone or porterhouse)
salt and pepper to taste
¼ teaspoon garlic powder *(optional)*

Set oven to broil. Place steak on pan. Add seasoning and put pan in broiler. Brown top of steak. Turn over and brown underside. Remove steak from broiler when cooked to your liking.

MOM'S STEAK DINNER

(4 servings)

INGREDIENTS

2 pounds steak (rib eye, sirloin or strip)
1 large onion, peeled and sliced in rings
1 green pepper, cleaned and sliced
1 cup ketchup
2 garlic cloves, minced or 1 teaspoon garlic powder
½ to 1 cup cold water
2 tablespoons oil
½ teaspoon salt
¼ teaspoon pepper

Cut steak into chunks. Heat oil in large frying pan. Place cut-up steak in hot oil and brown. Season steak with salt, pepper, and garlic. Add green peppers and onions. Pour ketchup over top. Add water to thin the ketchup sauce. Cover. Stir occasionally and heat until vegetables are medium soft. Keep warm until ready to serve.

FRIED STEAK

(2 servings)

INGREDIENTS

1 pound steak (T-bone, porterhouse, strip, rib eye)
1 tablespoon oil
salt and pepper to taste
¼ teaspoon garlic powder *(optional)*

On medium-high heat, sear steak in hot frying pan, browning both sides. Use small amount of oil in pan if it is not a non-stick pan. Season with salt, pepper, and garlic powder. Lower heat and fry steak slowly until cooked to your liking.

BEEF STEW

INGREDIENTS

2 pounds beef stew or shish kebab beef chunks
2 onions, chopped
2 cloves garlic, minced
1 cup flour
2 to 3 tablespoons shortening or oil
3 to 4 cups cold water
3 potatoes, peeled and cut into quarters
2 carrots, cut into large pieces
2 celery stalks, cut into large pieces
1 teaspoon salt
½ teaspoon pepper
1 teaspoon parsley flakes

Place chunks of beef in paper bag with flour. Shake bag, coating meat. In skillet, sauté onion and garlic in shortening. Add beef and brown. Add cold water, potatoes, carrots, celery, parsley, salt, and pepper. Simmer covered on medium heat until beef is tender, about 1½ hours. Turn heat down if sauce begins to boil too fast. Add more water if sauce gets too thick.

ROAST BEEF

INGREDIENTS

2½ to 3 pounds beef roast (sirloin tip, rump roast, or standing rib roast)
salt and pepper *(optional)*

Place beef in roasting pan, uncovered, and put in preheated 400° oven. Roast approximately 20 minutes per pound. If you prefer meat rare or well-done, alter the cooking time. Remove roast and slice thin. Serve with Quick Gravy (see p. 109).

(more time required to prepare this recipe)

INGREDIENTS—PART I

1 cup flour
1½ teaspoons baking powder
½ teaspoon salt
¼ teaspoon pepper
1 tablespoon oil
¼ cup water
8 ounces pork tenderloin, cut in chunks

Sift flour and baking powder. Add salt and pepper. Place oil in a bowl. Slowly add dry ingredients to oil with a small amount of water and stir until thick and smooth. Cut pork into cubes and dip each into the above batter. Fry meat in wok until fully cooked. Set aside. Pour out excess oil.

INGREDIENTS—PART II

2 tablespoons oil
1 onion, sliced
1 green pepper, sliced
1 small can pineapple chunks
2 tablespoons cornstarch or flour
½ cup light brown sugar
6 tablespoons pineapple juice
½ cup cider or rice vinegar
1 clove garlic, crushed or ½ teaspoon garlic powder
salt to taste
1 teaspoon fresh ginger, grated
6 tablespoons ketchup

Add oil to wok and heat. Add onion, peppers, and pineapple. Cook a short time until slightly softened. Remove and set aside. Mix all of the remaining ingredients together and cook in wok until it becomes thick. Simmer a few minutes. Add vegetables and pork to sauce and mix. Heat until all is warm. Serve.

PORK FONDUE

INGREDIENTS

1 pound pork fondue (cut in small chunks)
2 tablespoons oil
¼ cup flour
¼ to ½ cup water
¼ teaspoon garlic powder *(optional)*
½ teaspoon salt
¼ teaspoon pepper

Heat oil in frying pan. Add pork fondue. Salt and pepper to taste. Sprinkle flour (and garlic powder) over pork. Fry meat until slightly browned. Add a small amount of water to keep food from sticking to pan. Lower heat and cover with a lid. Simmer until pork is cooked through. Add enough water to make a sauce.

FRIED PORK CHOPS

(pork chops sliced thin fry quicker)

INGREDIENTS

6 pork chops
salt and pepper to taste
1 tablespoon oil

If pan is not teflon, rub oil on bottom of pan. If using a nonstick pan, place pork chops on dry, hot frying pan. Sprinkle salt and pepper on chops and fry until brown. Turn over and brown underside. Reduce heat and fry chops until cooked through. Do not undercook pork.

Suggestion: Use recipe for Brown Noodles (p. 62) and serve with pork chops.

INGREDIENTS

2½ to 3 pounds pork loin, center cut, or rib roast
1 teaspoon salt
½ teaspoon pepper
1 pint apple sauce

Sprinkle salt and pepper on roast. Place in a dry roasting pan fat side up, uncovered, in a hot 400° oven. Roast pork 1½ to 1¾ hours (about 30 minutes per pound). Cover roast with lid or foil if it starts to get too brown. Uncover roast for 10 minutes before removing from oven if you prefer a crisp outer layer. Serve with apple sauce.

─SMOKED SAUSAGE & SAUERKRAUT─

INGREDIENTS

1 pound smoked sausage
1 (27 oz.) can sauerkraut, drained
cold water

Drain juice from can of sauerkraut. Cut smoked sausage into large chunks. Place sauerkraut and smoked sausage in a pot. Add enough cold water to cover and place a lid on top. Simmer for 20 to 30 minutes.

Note: If desired, wieners may be added 5 minutes before removing from heat.

BAKED HAM

INGREDIENTS

½ semi-boneless precooked ham

Place ham in shallow pan (on rack if available). Place in warmed 325° oven for 45 minutes to 1 hour or until ham is heated through. Remove ham from oven and put on plate. Slice thin for sandwiches, or thicker for dinner.

Suggestion: To use leftover ham and bone, use recipe for Ham and Barley (below).

HAM & BARLEY

INGREDIENTS

1 pound ham (chunk, sliced, or ham bone)
1 cup barley
½ teaspoon garlic powder
½ teaspoon salt

Rinse 1 cup barley in cold water. Drain water. Place ham and barley in medium-sized heavy pot. Fill pot with cold water completely covering barley and ham. Add garlic powder and salt. Simmer. Cook for approximately 1 hour until barley is soft and water is slightly thickened. Add water if it gets too thick. Stir often to keep barley from sticking to sides and bottom of pot.

BARBECUED RIBS

INGREDIENTS

2 pounds pork spare ribs
1 quart barbecue sauce

Place ribs in roasting pan. Bake uncovered at 350° for 1 hour, turning to brown both sides. If ribs start to get too brown, cover them with a lid or foil. Remove from oven and pour grease out. Pour barbecue sauce (see p. 108) over ribs. Cover and return pan to oven for 20 to 30 minutes.

BAKED MACARONI & CHEESE

INGREDIENTS

3 cups cooked elbow macaroni
6 tablespoons butter
4 tablespoons flour
1 teaspoon salt
2 cups milk
2 cups American or Cheddar cheese, shredded
½ cup fine dry bread crumbs

Cook macaroni according to package directions. Set aside. Melt 4 tablespoons butter, add flour, and salt. Stir until smooth. Add milk. Cook and stir, keeping mixture smooth as it thickens. Add cheese. Mix well as cheese melts. In buttered casserole, place half of the cooked macaroni. Pour half of the sauce on top. Add another layer of macaroni, and repeat layering as above until all is used. Top with bread crumbs that have been mixed with 2 tablespoons melted butter. Bake at 350° for 30 minutes.

STUFFED SHELLS

INGREDIENTS

1 (12 oz.) box jumbo macaroni shells
8 ounces sharp or mild Cheddar cheese, shredded
12 ounces ricotta cheese
12 ounces mozzarella cheese, shredded
1 teaspoon parsley flakes
¾ teaspoon oregano or Italian seasoning
½ cup Parmesan cheese, grated
2 quarts spaghetti sauce
3 eggs
½ teaspoon salt
¼ teaspoon pepper

Cook shells according to box directions. Using two 9" by 13" by 2" cake pans, place small amount of sauce in bottoms of pans, enough to keep shells from sticking. Combine ricotta, Cheddar, mozzarella cheeses, eggs, parsley flakes, oregano, salt, and pepper in a large bowl and mix well. Fill shells with cheese mixture and place them open side down, filling both pans. Pour remaining spaghetti sauce over filled shells. Sprinkle grated Parmesan cheese over all. Bake covered with foil at 325° for 1 hour. Serves a large group.

FETTUCCINE ALFREDO

INGREDIENTS

1 (8 oz.) package egg noodles
¼ teaspoon salt
⅛ teaspoon pepper
¼ cup butter, melted
¼ cup Parmesan cheese, grated
2 tablespoons light cream or ricotta cheese

Cook noodles according to package directions and drain. While noodles are cooking, warm serving dish. In small bowl, combine butter, cheese, cream or ricotta cheese, salt, and pepper. Combine noodles and cheese mixture until coated and serve immediately. More Parmesan cheese may be added if desired.

GARLIC SPAGHETTI WITH BROCCOLI

INGREDIENTS

1 pound thin spaghetti
½ pound butter
1 box frozen or ½ bunch broccoli, washed
and cut in pieces
1 teaspoon salt
½ teaspoon pepper
2 tablespoons garlic powder
Parmesan cheese, grated *(optional)*

Melt butter in large skillet. Add broccoli, salt, pepper, and garlic powder and simmer until broccoli is cooked but firm. Cook spaghetti in boiling water according to package directions. After spaghetti is cooked, strained, and rinsed, add it to the broccoli mixture and stir. Add more salt, pepper or garlic powder if desired. Top with Parmesan cheese.

SHRIMP SCAMPI

INGREDIENTS

1 to 2 pounds fresh shelled deveined,
or thawed frozen shrimp
3 to 4 cloves garlic, crushed or 1 teaspoon garlic powder
½ cup butter
1 tablespoon lemon juice
¼ teaspoon salt
⅛ teaspoon pepper
½ teaspoon Italian seasoning
¼ cup parsley flakes
½ cup bread crumbs
1 lemon, cut in wedges

Heat shrimp in butter in a frying pan. Add remaining ingredients after shrimp turns pink. Simmer a few minutes, adding a little water if sauce gets too thick. Serve with lemon wedges.

BAKED FISH

INGREDIENTS

1 pound fish (sole, orange roughy, cod)
salt and pepper to taste
1 tablespoon butter
1 teaspoon lemon juice
1 onion, sliced *(optional)*
½ teaspoon garlic powder *(optional)*

Preheat oven to 350°. Place fish in a baking dish. Add salt and pepper. Dot with butter and sprinkle with lemon juice. Add onion slices and/or sprinkle garlic powder on top. Cover with lid or foil and bake until fish is white and flaky, approximately 10 minutes.

CHEESY FISH

INGREDIENTS

2 pounds fresh (or defrosted frozen) fish filets
½ cup salad dressing, Italian or Caesar
1 cup cornflakes, crushed
½ cup sharp Cheddar cheese, grated

Dip filets in salad dressing. Place them in a single layer in a baking dish. Combine cornflake crumbs and cheese and sprinkle over fish. Bake covered at 450° for 10 to 15 minutes or until fish flakes easily.

BEER BATTER FISH

INGREDIENTS

2 pounds fish (sole, herring, or other favorite)
2 cups flour
4 eggs
2 teaspoon salt
1 cup beer
½ cup oil

In a small bowl, mix all the above ingredients—except the oil and fish—until smooth. Dip the rinsed fish in batter, and deep fry in oil.

Note: Other varieties of fish or vegetables such as broccoli, mushrooms, and cauliflower can be prepared in this manner.

Soups, Salads, Vegetables & Side Dishes

CREAMY BROCCOLI SOUP

(5 servings)

INGREDIENTS

1 tablespoon butter or margarine
¼ cup onion, chopped
2 cups milk
8 ounces cream cheese
¾ pound processed cheese
1 package frozen chopped broccoli, drained
¼ teaspoon nutmeg

In medium-sized pot, melt shortening. Add onions and cook until soft. Add milk and cream cheese. Lower heat and cook until cream cheese melts. Add processed cheese, broccoli, and nutmeg. Heat slowly and mix to keep from sticking or burning. When broccoli is soft, soup is ready to eat.

QUICK CREAM OF SPINACH SOUP

INGREDIENTS

1 (10½ oz.) can cream of chicken soup
1 cup milk
1 (10 oz.) box frozen, chopped spinach

Thaw spinach ahead of time and squeeze out liquid. In a small heavy pot, combine chicken soup and milk and heat slowly. (Do not burn.) Add spinach. Heat and serve.

S
O
U
P
S

INGREDIENTS

4 to 5 pounds chicken, any parts (necks and backs
are less expensive; breasts can be used for
chicken salad [see p. 49] after soup is made)
5 quarts cold water
3 carrots, pared
2 stalks celery, washed
1 whole onion
3 cloves garlic
small bunch parsley, washed
1 teaspoon salt
½ teaspoon pepper

Wash chicken in cold water. Place chicken in large pot.
Add approximately 5 quarts cold water and remaining
ingredients. Cover and cook at a slow boil for 3 hours.
Skim fat from top with spoon or paper towel. When
cooked, use colander to strain soup. Cool and refrigerate. Fat will come to the top if refrigerated overnight.
Remove fat before reheating to serve. Add cooked
noodles or dumplings (see p. 45) to soup.

Note: If eaten soon after cooked, fat can be removed
from the top more quickly by wrapping an ice cube in
a clean cloth (or paper towel) and dipping it in the
soup. The fat will adhere to the cloth.

Variation: Substitute cubed chuck to make beef soup
broth.

DUMPLINGS FOR SOUP

INGREDIENTS

2 to 3 eggs
¾ to 1¼ cups flour
½ teaspoon salt
¼ teaspoon pepper

In small bowl, beat eggs very well with fork. Add flour, starting with ½ cup and continue beating. Keep adding flour until batter is the consistency of thick pudding. Add salt and pepper. To cook, drop one tablespoon of batter at a time into slowly boiling broth. Simmer until dumplings come to the surface of the boiling broth.

VINAIGRETTE SALAD

INGREDIENTS

1 head lettuce *(optional)*
2 to 3 tomatoes, sliced
1 teaspoon wine vinegar
2 tablespoons salad oil
½ teaspoon sugar
½ teaspoon oregano flakes
½ teaspoon salt
¼ teaspoon pepper
parsley flakes for garnish

Place tomatoes and lettuce on large plate. Combine all remaining ingredients in small bowl and stir. Pour dressing over vegetables and garnish with parsley flakes.

COMBINATION SALAD WITH DRESSING

INGREDIENTS

½ head lettuce, cleaned and torn
1 cucumber, peeled and sliced
1 tomato, cut in wedges
1 small onion, peeled and cut in rings
½ teaspoon salt
¼ teaspoon pepper
½ teaspoon Italian seasoning
¼ teaspoon sugar *(optional)*
1 tablespoon wine vinegar
1 tablespoon vegetable oil

Wash vegetables in cold water. Set aside to drain. In large bowl, combine all of the above ingredients and mix. Add more salt to taste.

GREEK SALAD

INGREDIENTS

1 medium head lettuce, cut up
2 tomatoes, cut in wedges
¾ cup feta cheese
1 small green onion, sliced
1 (2 oz.) can drained anchovies
⅔ cup oil, olive or vegetable
⅓ cup wine vinegar
½ teaspoon salt
⅛ teaspoon pepper
¼ teaspoon dried oregano

Combine oil, vinegar, salt, pepper, oregano, and mix well. Pour over salad made up of the remaining ingredients.

LEBANESE SALAD

(6 to 8 servings)

INGREDIENTS

1 head lettuce, cleaned and drained
2 tomatoes
8 Greek oil-cured olives
2 tablespoons dried oregano
2 tablespoons mint leaves, crumbled
1 tablespoon oil
1 tablespoon vinegar
1 tablespoon lemon juice
salt and pepper to taste

In bowl, place lettuce which has been broken up (not cut up) in pieces. Cut tomatoes in eighths and add to bowl. Add the remaining ingredients and toss.

QUICK SPINACH SALAD

INGREDIENTS

⅓ cup salad oil
2 teaspoons lemon juice
2 teaspoons cider vinegar
3 teaspoons sugar
1 hard-boiled egg
1 package frozen spinach, defrosted and
drained or fresh, clean spinach
2 to 3 slices crisp fried bacon, crumbled

In small bowl, blend first four ingredients. Chill. In large bowl, combine spinach with the contents of the smaller bowl and mix well. Add chopped egg. Sprinkle bacon on top.

MACARONI SALAD

INGREDIENTS

1 pound sea shells or spring macaroni, cooked
as directed on package
1 can pitted black olives, cut in halves
1 jar green olives with pimento, cut in halves
1 tomato, cubed
1 cucumber, sliced
1 small onion, chopped
1 package Italian dressing, mixed
according to package directions

Combine all of the above ingredients and mix well. Refrigerate until ready to serve. Mix before serving.

COLESLAW

INGREDIENTS

½ head cabbage, shredded
2 tablespoons white vinegar
2 tablespoons oil
salt and pepper to taste
½ teaspoon sugar *(optional)*

Place the above ingredients in a bowl and mix together.

CHICKEN SALAD

INGREDIENTS

1 cooked chicken breast, boned and
skinned; cut into chunks
1 stalk celery, chopped
½ cup mayonnaise for blending
salt and pepper to taste *(optional)*

In small bowl, combine all of the above and mix. Chill.

HEAD LETTUCE MAYO

INGREDIENTS

1 wedge lettuce
1 tablespoon mayonnaise
½ tomato *(optional)*
½ green pepper *(optional)*

Wash head of lettuce in cold water. Drain. Place wedge of lettuce on serving plate. Top with mayonnaise. Add tomato wedges and green pepper slices if desired.

POTATO SALAD

INGREDIENTS

6 potatoes (boiled in skins) peeled and cubed
2 hard-boiled eggs, peeled and cut up
1 stalk celery, chopped
½ cup mayonnaise
salt and pepper *(optional)*

Combine all of the above ingredients. Mix and refrigerate. Do not cut potatoes too small as they will get mushy when they are mixed. More or less mayonnaise may be used. If you are calorie conscious, use less mayonnaise or the light variety.

TUNA SALAD

INGREDIENTS

1 (6½ oz.) can tuna, preferably white tuna in spring water
1 stalk celery, chopped
½ cup mayonnaise, or enough to blend
green grapes *(optional)*
raisins *(optional)*

In small bowl, place drained and flaked tuna. Add celery. Add enough mayonnaise to blend. Add grapes or raisins if desired.

BAKED STUFFED TOMATOES

INGREDIENTS

6 medium ripe tomatoes
½ cup butter
1 cup bread crumbs
1 tablespoon parsley flakes
1 teaspoon salt
⅛ teaspoon pepper
1 tablespoon sugar
2 tablespoons vinegar
2 tablespoons water

In small pan melt butter. Add bread crumbs, parsley, salt, and pepper. Mix and set aside. Remove stem ends from tomatoes. In shallow baking dish, place tomatoes with stem side down. Cut tomatoes in quarters halfway through. Do not cut through to bottom. In small bowl, combine sugar, salt, pepper, vinegar, and water. Mix. Spoon mixture into each tomato. Bake about 30 minutes at 325° or until tomatoes are slightly soft. Remove from oven and top with butter-crumb mixture. Place tomatoes under broiler for about 2 minutes or until lightly browned.

BAKED BEANS

INGREDIENTS

1 (16 oz.) can pork and beans or
vegetarian beans in tomato sauce
1 tablespoon brown sugar
2 to 3 slices bacon *(optional)*

Cut bacon in small pieces and fry in a skillet until crisp. Add beans and brown sugar. Mix and heat.

CREAMED PEAS

Ingredients

2 tablespoons butter
2 tablespoons flour
1 cup cold milk
1 (16 oz.) can peas
½ teaspoon salt
¼ teaspoon pepper
½ cup onion, chopped fine

In frying pan, melt butter. Add flour and onions and mix continuously. Add a very small amount of milk to make thickening. Stir until smooth and onions are soft. Mix slowly while adding remaining milk. When slightly thickened, add drained peas and heat until peas are hot.

SEASONED GREEN BEANS

Ingredients

1 (15 oz.) can green beans or 1 pound fresh green beans
2 tablespoons butter
¼ teaspoon Italian seasoning
½ teaspoon garlic powder
salt and pepper to taste

If using fresh green beans, remove end stems and wash in cold water. Heat and soften beans in ½ cup cold water. Drain. If using canned beans, drain liquid. Heat beans in butter. Add salt, pepper, Italian seasoning, and garlic powder. Heat and stir beans until hot.

GREEN BEANS AMANDINE

INGREDIENTS

1 large package frozen french-style green beans
½ stick butter
¼ cup slivered almonds
salt and pepper to taste

Defrost and drain beans. In a frying pan, brown almonds lightly in butter. Add beans to almonds. Heat and stir. Add salt and pepper as desired.

GARLIC SPINACH

INGREDIENTS

1 pound fresh spinach, washed, drained,
and heated in water until soft, or 1 box frozen
spinach, defrosted, liquid drained
½ teaspoon garlic powder
1 tablespoon oil
salt and pepper to taste

Place all of the above ingredients in a pan. Heat and mix well.

BUTTERED MUSHROOMS

INGREDIENTS

1 pound mushrooms
2 to 3 tablespoons butter
½ teaspoon salt
¼ teaspoon pepper
¼ teaspoon garlic powder
¼ teaspoon parsley flakes

Wash fresh mushrooms in cold water. Heat them in a pan with butter. Add salt, pepper, garlic powder, and parsley flakes. Stir and heat slowly until mushrooms are warm and soft, approximately 3 minutes.

V
E
G
E
T
A
B
L
E
S

Ingredients

1 (14 oz.) can sliced beets, drained
1 small onion, sliced
1 tablespoon white vinegar
1 tablespoon oil
salt and pepper to taste
pinch of sugar *(optional)*

In small bowl, mix all of the above ingredients together.

──────── HOME FRIED POTATOES ────────

Ingredients

4 potatoes, unpeeled
¼ cup oil
paprika *(optional)*
salt to taste

Wash potatoes in cold water. Place potatoes in pot and cover with cold water. Boil potatoes in skins until tender when pricked with a fork. Drain water. Peel and dice potatoes. Heat oil in a frying pan until hot. Add potatoes and fry, turning often until golden brown. Sprinkle lightly with paprika and turn them over a few times before removing them from pan. Add salt to taste.

Note: Unpeeled cooked potatoes may be refrigerated and fried at a later time.

MASHED POTATOES

INGREDIENTS

6 potatoes
½ teaspoon salt
water, enough to cover potatoes
½ stick butter
⅓ cup milk

Wash potatoes in cold water. Cut potatoes in large chunks or cubes. Place them in a pot of salted cold water and cook. Bring to boil, cover and simmer until potatoes are tender. Drain water and mash potatoes with electric mixer or potato masher until smooth. Add butter and milk. Mix well. Add more salt if necessary. Leftover mashed potatoes can easily be heated in microwave or made into Potato Patties (see p. 58).

BAKED POTATOES

2 potatoes
4 tablespoons butter *(optional)*
4 ounces sour cream *(optional)*
salt *(optional)*

Wash potatoes in cold water. Wrap each potato in foil. Prick potato with knife or fork through foil and potato skin to allow steam to escape. Bake potatoes at 400° until soft when squeezed by hand or pricked with fork. Baking time will be determined by the size of the potato, approximately 1 to 1½ hours. Serve with butter or sour cream.

COOKED RED POTATOES

INGREDIENTS

4 red potatoes, unpeeled
½ teaspoon salt
½ teaspoon pepper
¼ teaspoon garlic powder
1 tablespoon oil
¼ teaspoon parsley flakes

Wash unpeeled potatoes. Place potatoes in pot and add enough cold water to cover potatoes. Cook until soft. Do not overcook or they will be mushy. Drain water. Cool. Cut potatoes in eighths. Do not remove skins. Add salt, pepper, and garlic powder. Mix all with oil and parsley flakes. Serve warm or cold.

POTATOES WITH SOUR CREAM

INGREDIENTS

6 to 8 potatoes
¾ cup butter
1 small onion, chopped
1 pint sour cream
½ teaspoon chopped parsley

Wash, peel, and cube potatoes. Place potatoes in a baking dish. Melt butter and pour over potatoes. Add onion and stir to coat potatoes. Cover and bake until soft. Remove from oven. Add sour cream and parsley. Mix and serve.

SCALLOPED POTATOES

INGREDIENTS

4 large or 6 medium potatoes
1 small onion, chopped
1 (10¾ oz.) can soup (cream of mushroom or
cream of chicken)
¾ cup milk

Wash, peel, and slice potatoes. Place in a baking dish or pan. Add chopped onion and soup. Add milk to prevent it from becoming too thick. Place in oven, cover and bake at 325° until potatoes are soft, approximately 30 to 45 minutes. Add more milk if sauce gets too thick.

57

POTATO PATTIES

INGREDIENTS

1 cup mashed potatoes
1 tablespoon butter

Make patties out of leftover mashed potatoes. (Place waxed paper between layered patties to keep them from sticking together.) Fry patties in a buttered skillet. Turn with spatula to brown both sides.

BAKED YAMS

INGREDIENTS

2 medium yams
2 tablespoons butter

Wash potatoes in cold water. Prick outer skin with fork to allow steam to escape. Bake in oven at 350° until soft, about 1 to 1½ hours depending on size. Remove from oven. Cut potatoes in half. Top with butter.

MASHED YAMS

INGREDIENTS

4 yams
½ stick butter

Wash potatoes in cold water. Prick outer skin with a fork to allow steam to escape. Bake potatoes approximately 1 to 1½ hours at 350° until tender when squeezed or pricked with a fork. Remove from oven. Cut potato skins in half; remove pulp. Place pulp and butter in bowl and mash with potato masher or electric mixer.

BAKED ORANGE YAMS

(6 to 8 servings)

INGREDIENTS

6 to 8 yams
1 stick butter
¼ cup brown sugar
½ cup orange juice

Wash potatoes in cold water and remove peels. Cut potatoes in quarters lengthwise and place in baking dish. Cut butter in pieces and scatter over the potatoes. Sprinkle with brown sugar. Pour orange juice over all. Bake at 325° covered until soft, about 1 hour. Using a large spoon, baste the potatoes occasionally while baking. The juice will flavor the potatoes.

CORNMEAL POLENTA

INGREDIENTS

1 cup yellow cornmeal
2 cups water
½ teaspoon salt
1 cup sour cream
1 cup creamed cottage cheese
¼ pound butter
2 green onions, chopped
4 slices bacon *(optional)*

In heavy pot, boil water. Add salt. Gradually add cornmeal and stir. Cover and lower heat. Allow to heat for approximately 30 minutes stirring occasionally. In bowl, mix sour cream and cottage cheese together. Set aside. In small pan, melt butter. Add green onions. Simmer and brown slightly. To serve, place polenta on a plate. Spread sour cream mixture over it. Top with browned onions. Crisp crumbled bacon may be used on top.

VEGETABLES & SIDE DISHES

BREAD STUFFING

(for turkey or chicken)

INGREDIENTS

½ cup chicken fat or ½ cup butter
1½ cups chopped celery
1 large onion, chopped
2 eggs
2 tablespoons parsley
2 cloves garlic, finely chopped
1½ teaspoons salt
¾ teaspoon pepper
21 ounces dry bread cubes or stuffing mix
1 pound mushrooms *(optional)*

In large skillet over low heat, soften celery, onion, parsley, garlic, and mushroom pieces in chicken fat or butter and water. Add salt, pepper, dry bread, and mix. Remove from heat. In bowl, place two eggs and beat well. Add eggs to bread mixture and mix well. Stuff turkey or chicken immediately before roasting. If stuffing is made in advance, refrigerate it. Do not stuff chicken or turkey unless you are ready to bake it. Stuffing can also be baked separately in covered casserole, at 325° for 1 hour.

CHICKEN-FLAVORED RICE

INGREDIENTS

½ cup rice, cooked as directed on package
1 can chicken rice soup

Combine drained cooked rice and chicken rice soup. Heat and serve.

FLUFFY RICE

INGREDIENTS

1 cup long grain rice
2 cups cold water
1 tablespoon butter *(optional)*
pinch of salt

In a medium pot, combine and heat all of the above ingredients. Reduce the heat when it begins to simmer. Stir. Cover and cook about 20 minutes or until all of the water is absorbed and rice is tender.* Do not burn. Rice is very good served with stir-fry chicken, or milk and sugar may be added to individual servings of rice.

* more water may be added if necessary

LEMON RICE

INGREDIENTS

1 cup cooked long grain rice (follow package directions for cooking)
3 cups chicken broth
1 tablespoon lemon peel, grated fine
2 tablespoons butter, melted
¼ teaspoon salt
⅛ teaspoon pepper

Combine all of the above ingredients. Heat and mix. Add salt and pepper to taste.

CHEESY NOODLES

S
I
D
E

D
I
S
H
E
S

Ingredients

1 pound cooked, drained noodles
1 pound cottage cheese, drained
4 egg yolks
½ cup sour cream
1 teaspoon salt
¼ cup bread crumbs
4 tablespoons melted butter

Cook noodles according to package directions. Set aside. In bowl, combine first four ingredients and beat until smooth. In buttered baking dish, alternate layers of noodles and cheese mixture, starting and ending with noodles. Sprinkle with bread crumbs and melted butter. Bake at 375° for 30 minutes.

BROWN NOODLES

Ingredients

8 ounce bag wide egg noodles
pan drippings and brown crusty remains
from frying pork chops

Boil noodles in salted water according to package directions. Place noodles in pan from which fried pork chops were removed while remaining grease and drippings are still hot. Mix noodles around in the pan until they are coated brown. Add more salt and pepper if necessary.

Note: If you do not have pork chop drippings, combine cooked noodles with one stick melted butter and mix. Noodles will remain white but tasty. Garlic powder can be added if desired.

Breakfasts

EGG-CHEESE CASSEROLE

(8 servings–can be prepared the day before)

INGREDIENTS

8 ounces grated sharp Cheddar cheese or cheese
of your choice
6 eggs, beaten
1 package smoked links or ham cut into pieces
¼ teaspoon salt
⅛ teaspoon pepper
1 teaspoon dry mustard
6 slices bread, cubed
2 cups milk

Combine all of the above ingredients and place in a casserole. Refrigerate overnight. Bake at 350° for 1 hour.

SCRAMBLED EGGS

INGREDIENTS

2 eggs
salt and pepper
2 to 3 tablespoons milk *(optional)*
1 or 2 slices American or Cheddar cheese *(optional)*

Crack eggs into a small bowl. Sprinkle lightly with salt and pepper. Beat eggs with fork or wire whisk until whites and yolks are well-blended. Melt 1 teaspoon butter in warm frying pan. Add eggs and cook on medium heat. Stir eggs to keep them from sticking to pan. Remove from pan when fluffy.

Variation 1: Add 2 to 3 tablespoons milk to eggs before scrambling for fluffier eggs.

Variation 2: Add a slice of cheese to eggs and mix in while cooking.

65

**B
R
E
A
K
F
A
S
T
S**

INGREDIENTS

eggs
salt and pepper
water

Place eggs in pan and cover with cold water. Bring water to a boil. Remove eggs from heat. Cover and allow them to stand approximately 15 minutes. Pour out hot water and rinse eggs in cold water. Peel shells and season eggs.

SOFT-BOILED EGGS

INGREDIENTS

eggs
salt and pepper
water

Place eggs in pan and cover with cold water. Place pan on burner and heat, bringing water to a boil. Remove pan from heat and cover. Allow eggs to remain in the water for 1½ to 2 minutes. Drain hot water and rinse eggs in cold water. Peel shells and season eggs.

POACHED EGGS

INGREDIENTS

eggs
1 teaspoon butter *(optional)*
salt and pepper

Crack eggs into ½ inch slowly simmering water. If any other than nonstick pan is used, rub bottom of pan with butter before putting water in the pan. After underside of egg is molded, pour tablespoonfuls of the remaining hot water over the top side of the eggs, basting them. Eggs are cooked when whites are firm. Remove from water with a spatula or slotted spoon.

B
R
E
A
K
F
A
S
T
S

eggs
salt and pepper
1 teaspoon butter

Melt butter on low heat in frying pan. Crack egg-shells and gently drop eggs into pan. Fry eggs slowly. When almost cooked, place a lid on the skillet or baste top side of eggs with the melted butter in which the eggs are cooking. If eggs are fried too fast, the under-side and edges may turn brown. Eggs are cooked when whites are firm.

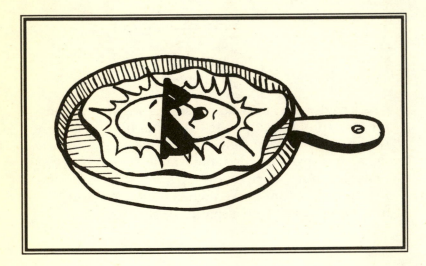

EGGS-OVER

INGREDIENTS

eggs
1 teaspoon butter
salt and pepper

Heat 1 teaspoon butter in frying pan. Crack eggshells and gently drop eggs into pan. Fry eggs slowly. When eggs are almost cooked, turn them over carefully with a spatula. Allow to cook a few seconds and gently remove from pan.

HAM AND CHEESE OMELET

INGREDIENTS

3 to 4 eggs
diced ham
shredded cheese
1 teaspoon butter
salt and pepper

Crack eggs into a small bowl and whisk until blended. Melt butter in skillet. Pour eggs into skillet and heat. Cook slowly until top is set. Cover half with ham and cheese. Fold other half over and serve.

PORK SAUSAGE LINKS

INGREDIENTS

pork links

Place links in a frying pan. Add enough water to cover bottom of pan. Cook links until water evaporates. Links will turn pale as they are cooked in water. Continue to fry and turn them after the water is gone. When they are slightly browned, they are ready to serve.

BAKED BACON

(baking saves time for large amount of bacon)

INGREDIENTS

1 pound bacon

Place bacon on broiling pan about 4 inches from heating element. Separate slices. Bake at 350 to 400°, turning slices as they become crisp and browned. Remove from oven and place bacon on paper bag or paper towels to absorb excess grease.

FRIED BACON

INGREDIENTS

6 to 8 slices bacon

Separate bacon slices and place them side by side on a hot skillet. Turn slices as they become crisp. After browned, remove bacon from pan and place the strips on absorbent paper to remove excess grease.

Note: Bacon slices are separated more easily if the bacon is removed from the refrigerator 30 minutes before frying.

CHEESY TOAST

INGREDIENTS

2 slices bread
1 tablespoon butter
1 cup shredded cheese (American,
Cheddar, or mozzarella)

Toast bread. Butter top sides of toast. Add thick layer of cheese, covering all edges. Place toast on baking tray or aluminum foil. Broil 4 inches from heating unit until cheese melts. Remove from oven.

CINNAMON TOAST

INGREDIENTS

2 slices bread
2 teaspoons butter
1 teaspoon cinnamon
½ teaspoon sugar

Toast bread. Butter toast. Sprinkle cinnamon and sugar on top.

Note: Cinnamon-sugar can be purchased already mixed together in the spice department of your grocery store.

ONE-MINUTE OATMEAL

INGREDIENTS

1 cup dry 1-minute oatmeal
cold water
¼ teaspoon salt *(optional)*
½ cup milk
sugar to taste

Place oatmeal in a small pan. Add enough cold water to cover. Heat to simmer and stir. Add salt if desired. Cook until very hot and slightly thickened. Serve with granulated sugar and milk.

QUICK PANCAKES

INGREDIENTS

2 cups pancake flour mix or Bisquick
2 eggs
1 cup milk
1 teaspoon butter
½ cup maple syrup

Combine flour, eggs, and milk. Mix well. Heat griddle or frying pan and rub with 1 teaspoon butter. Place 1 or 2 tablespoonfuls of batter on griddle to form pancakes, making them any desired size. When bubbles appear on top of the cooking pancakes, turn them over and brown the other side. Serve with butter, margarine, preserves, jam, syrup, or topping of your choice.

FRENCH TOAST

INGREDIENTS

2 eggs
1 teaspoon butter
¼ cup milk
6 slices bread
maple syrup
butter

Whisk eggs in a small bowl. Add milk and mix well. Heat frying pan or griddle. Add 1 teaspoon butter to frying pan and melt, covering entire bottom of pan. Dip bread slices into egg batter one by one, covering them completely with batter. Place them on the hot griddle. Turn them over when underside is golden brown and brown the top side. Remove from heat and serve hot with butter and maple syrup or topping of your choice.

Sandwiches

TUNA MELT

(2 sandwiches)

INGREDIENTS

1 (6 oz.) can tuna, drained
4 slices bread
1 small onion, chopped
2 tablespoons butter
¼ teaspoon salt *(optional)*
⅛ teaspoon pepper *(optional)*
2 slices American or Swiss cheese
2 to 4 tablespoons mayonnaise
lettuce and tomato *(optional)*

Butter one side of each slice of bread. Drain liquid from tuna. In small pan combine tuna, mayonnaise, onion, salt, and pepper. Mix and heat the tuna mixture. On griddle, place 2 slices of bread, butter side down. Place half of tuna mixture on each slice of bread. Top each with 1 slice of cheese. Add second slice of bread with butter side up. Turn sandwich over and toast. Cheese should be melted. Serve.

S
A
N
D
W
I
C
H
E
S

QUICK SLOPPY JOES

(6 sandwiches)

INGREDIENTS

1 pound ground meat
1 package sloppy joe mix
1 (8 oz.) can tomato sauce
6 buns

In frying pan, brown ground meat. Add sloppy joe mix and stir. Add tomato sauce and mix. Simmer until hot. Add small amount of water if it gets too thick. Heat well and serve on buns.

CLUB OR COMBINATION SANDWICH

(1 sandwich)

INGREDIENTS

1 egg
2 slices ham
3 slices toast
2 slices cheese
lettuce
2 slices tomato
mayonnaise
1 teaspoon butter

On low heat, melt butter in skillet. Scramble egg. Remove egg and set aside. Place ham in same warm skillet and heat. Turn ham over and place scrambled egg on ham while still in skillet. Toast bread. Remove ham and egg combination from pan and place on a slice of toast, covering with a second slice. Put lettuce and tomato on top of second slice of toast. Cheese and mayonnaise or other condiments may be added. Slice sandwich into 4 diagonal wedges. Put a toothpick through each of the 4 sections to keep layers from falling apart.

HAM BARBECUE

(2 to 3 sandwiches)

Ingredients

½ pound chipped ham
½ pint barbecue sauce
2 to 3 buns

Heat chipped or thinly sliced ham in pot. Add prepared barbecue sauce and mix. Serve on bun.

——GRILLED CHEESE SANDWICH——

(1 sandwich)

INGREDIENTS

2 buttered slices of bread
2 to 3 slices American cheese

Place a slice of bread on warm frying pan or griddle, butter side down. Place cheese on top of bread. Top with second slice of bread, butter side up. Heat until underside of bread is toasted. Turn sandwich over and toast the other slice. Cheese should melt. If cheese is not melted, place a lid over the sandwich. Garnish with pickle or other condiments.

————————CHEESEBURGERS————————

(6 large sandwiches)

INGREDIENTS

1 pound ground beef
1 teaspoon oil *(optional)*
12 slices cheese
6 buns

Shape ground beef into patties. Place them on a hot frying pan or griddle. (Oil pan if it is not teflon.) Fry and brown both sides. Turn heat down and allow to cook until meat is done to desired taste. When fully cooked, top with 1 or 2 slices of cheese. Continue to heat until cheese is melted. Cheese will melt very quickly if a lid is used. Place patty on a bun and top with your choice of garnish.

Note: If broiling, use a thicker patty.

INGREDIENTS

wieners
buns
slices of cheese *(optional)*

To broil: Set oven on broil. Cut wieners in half length-wise and place in pan. Put pan in broiler and heat until wieners are slightly browned. Remove from broiler. (Top each wiener with a slice of cheese if desired.)

To boil: In small pan, add 1 inch cold water and heat to boil. Add wieners. Turn heat to medium and simmer 1 to 2 minutes until wieners are hot. Serve on buns.

REUBEN

(1 sandwich)

INGREDIENTS

¼ cup sauerkraut
1 slice turkey
1 slice corned beef
1 slice Swiss cheese
2 slices rye bread
1 tablespoon butter
2 to 3 tablespoons Russian dressing *(optional)*

Rinse sauerkraut in cold water. Squeeze out water. Butter 2 slices of rye bread. Place 1 slice, butter side down on hot frying pan. Top with corned beef, kraut, turkey, and cheese. Place second slice of bread on top with buttered side up. Toast bottom slice. Turn sandwich with spatula and toast other side. Remove from heat. Add Russian dressing.

BEEF BARBECUE

INGREDIENTS

1 pound ground beef
2 tablespoons oil
1 onion, chopped
1 cup tomato sauce
2 tablespoons brown sugar
1 tablespoon mustard
1 tablespoon Worcestershire sauce

In skillet, brown ground beef. Pour off fat and reserve meat in a bowl. In same pan, cook onion in oil until lightly browned. Add all of the other ingredients including the meat. Simmer about 20 minutes. Serve on hamburger buns.

Breads & Rolls

INGREDIENTS

1 cup flour
1 cup yellow cornmeal
¼ cup sugar
3 teaspoons baking powder
1 teaspoon salt
¼ cup shortening
1 cup milk
1 egg

Preheat oven to 425°. In large bowl, combine flour, cornmeal, sugar, baking powder, and salt. Mix well. Add shortening and mix with fork, breaking mixture into crumbs. In separate bowl, whisk egg with fork. Add milk and mix well. Add egg mixture to dry ingredients mixing slightly. Bake all in a greased 9 inch or comparable-sized baking pan for approximately 20 minutes. Corn bread is baked when toothpick inserted into bread comes out free of batter.

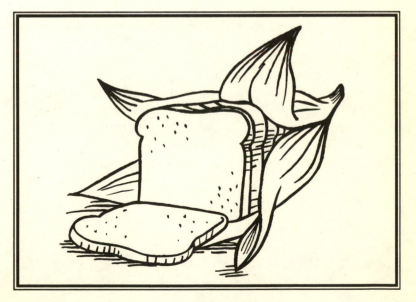

——FREEZER LOAF GARLIC BREAD——

INGREDIENTS

1 loaf french bread
½ cup butter, melted or softened
¼ teaspoon garlic powder
Parmesan cheese *(optional)*

Cut bread in thick slices but don't cut through to bottom of the loaf. In small bowl, mix butter and garlic powder together and spread over inside of cut bread slices. Sprinkle with Parmesan cheese. Wrap bread in foil and freeze. When ready to serve, open top of foil wrap and heat loaf on foil in which bread was wrapped, for 30 minutes at 375°. If the bread starts to get too brown, cover top of bread with more foil.

————SLICED GARLIC BREAD————

INGREDIENTS

1 loaf Italian or French bread, sliced thick
1 tablespoon garlic powder
1 stick butter, melted
Parmesan cheese *(optional)*

Combine melted butter and garlic powder. Spread garlic butter on both sides of bread. Place on aluminum foil or baking pan 6 inches away from upper heating element and toast. Turn bread over to toast the other side. Watch carefully as bread browns quickly. Sprinkle Parmesan cheese on top of toast, if desired.

BAGELS

B
R
E
A
D
S

&

R
O
L
L
S

Ingredients

4 to 4¼ cups flour
4 tablespoons sugar
1 cup hot water
2 packages dry rapid rise yeast
1 tablespoon salt

Fill large pot halfway with cold water. Add 1 table-spoon sugar and bring to boil. In large mixing bowl, combine flour, 3 tablespoons sugar, yeast, and salt. Mix. Add 1 cup hot water to flour mixture and mix to dough consistency. Separate dough mixture into 12 equal parts. Shape each part into bagel shape and poke hole in center. Place 12 bagels on greased cookie sheet and bake at 375° for 5 minutes on top shelf. Remove from oven and place bagels in boiling water for 5 minutes. Remove from water and place on same cookie sheet and bake until top side is light brown. Turn over and brown the other side.

Sweets

BLUEBERRY GELATIN MOLD

INGREDIENTS

½ teaspoon oil or nonstick cooking spray
1 (3 oz.) package blueberry gelatin
2 cups boiling water
1 pound can blueberry pie filling
1 (20 oz.) can crushed pineapple, including juice
½ cup pecans, crushed
topping (see p. 93)

If using mold, spray mold with nonstick cooking spray or rub lightly with oil. In medium-sized bowl, combine and mix gelatin and boiling water. Add pie filling and mix. Add pineapple and pecans. Mix well and pour into mold. Refrigerate until gelled. When ready to serve, spoon into individual serving bowls and top each with 2 tablespoons topping. To remove gelatin from mold, immerse mold in hot water for a few seconds. Place a plate on top of the mold and turn it over to release the gelatin.

CHERRY GELATIN SALAD

INGREDIENTS

1 (6 oz.) package cherry gelatin
1 large can pitted black cherries
1 pint sour cream
1 cup hot water
1 cup cold water
½ cup chopped pecans

In bowl, dissolve gelatin in 1 cup hot water and mix. After 2 minutes, add 1 cup cold water and mix. Refrigerate until slightly gelled. Remove from refrigerator. Add sour cream and blend well. Add cherries and pecans. Refrigerate.

——PISTACHIO PUDDING SALAD——

INGREDIENTS

1 (16 or 20 oz.) can crushed pineapple, undrained
2 cups miniature marshmallows
1 cup chopped walnuts or pecans
1 (3½ oz.) package instant dry pistachio pudding mix
1 (9 oz.) container whipped topping

In medium-sized bowl, combine all of the above ingredients. Mix well and refrigerate.

——STRAWBERRY YOGURT GELATIN——

INGREDIENTS

1 (3 oz.) box strawberry gelatin
1 cup boiling water
¾ cup cold water
1 (8 oz.) container strawberry yogurt

In medium bowl, dissolve gelatin in boiling water. After 2 minutes, add cold water and mix. Refrigerate until partially set. Remove from refrigerator and add yogurt, mixing well. Refrigerate.

——GELATIN WHIP——

INGREDIENTS

1 (3 oz.) box gelatin, any flavor
1 container whipped topping

Mix gelatin as directed on package. Cool to soupy texture. Add whipped topping and blend. Refrigerate.

WHITE CREAMY ICING

INGREDIENTS

½ cup butter
½ cup other shortening (i.e., margarine)
1 cup powdered sugar, packed
¼ cup warm milk
1 unbeaten egg
¾ teaspoon vanilla

Mix butter and other shortening together until creamy. Add sugar and mix. Add milk and mix. Add egg and mix. Add vanilla and mix.

LEMON GLAZE

(use on plain cake)

INGREDIENTS

1 lemon
1 to 1½ cups powdered sugar

Squeeze juice of lemon in small bowl or cup. Remove seeds. Add sugar and mix until slightly thickened. Add more sugar if necessary. Continue to mix until smooth. Pour over cake allowing it to drip down the sides.

TOPPING

INGREDIENTS

8 ounces cream cheese
8 ounces sour cream
½ cup sugar

In a small bowl, combine all of the above ingredients and mix well. Refrigerate. When serving, place heaping tablespoonful on each serving of dessert.

93

MARSHMALLOW ICING

INGREDIENTS

1½ cups sugar
½ cup water
3 egg whites
⅓ teaspoon cream of tartar
1 teaspoon vanilla

Combine sugar and cold water in small heavy pot and simmer until hard ball stage* (about 15 to 20 minutes). Beat egg whites in large bowl with electric mixer. Add sugar mixture to fluffy egg whites in a slow stream while beating at high speed. Add vanilla and cream of tartar until creamy. Mix well.

Note: To test for "hard ball stage": drop a small amount of sugar-water mixture into a small plate that has 2 to 3 tablespoons of cold water in it. The drop should stay together and not break apart. Move it with your finger to check. If it comes apart, allow mixture to cook longer.

INSTANT PUDDING FROSTING

INGREDIENTS

½ cup shortening of choice
1 stick (¼ pound) butter
1 cup sugar
1 (3½ oz.) box instant dry pudding, any flavor
1 cup milk

In bowl, combine shortening and butter. Cream well. Add sugar and mix. In another smaller bowl, mix together pudding and milk. Combine butter mixture with gelatin mixture. Mix well.

CHOCOLATE BUTTER CREAM FROSTING

INGREDIENTS

½ pound sweet unsalted butter
¾ to 1 box powdered sugar
1 whole egg
unsweetened cocoa, (approximately 1 tablespoon)
1 teaspoon vanilla

With electric mixer, cream butter. Slowly add sugar. Mix. Add egg and mix. Add cocoa. Taste and add more cocoa as desired. Add vanilla. Mix well. Frost cake.

GRAHAM CRACKER CRUST

INGREDIENTS

⅓ cup butter
2 tablespoons sugar
1¼ cups graham cracker crumbs

Combine sugar and melted butter. Add graham cracker crumbs and mix well. Add crumb mixture to pie pan and press it to the bottom and sides of the pan. Refrigerate.

Note: Fill graham cracker pie shell with your favorite filling. Instant dry puddings of all flavors made according to package directions are very good. Top with whipped cream or ready made whipped topping.

CARAMEL BROWNIES

INGREDIENTS

1 box German chocolate cake mix
¾ cup butter, melted
⅓ cup evaporated milk
50 light caramels
1 can milk chocolate frosting
⅓ cup evaporated milk
6 ounces semi-sweet chocolate chips
1 cup chopped nuts

In medium bowl, combine cake mix, butter and ⅓ cup evaporated milk. In a 9″ by 13″ pan, place half of the chocolate mixture in pan, covering the bottom. Bake for 6 minutes at 350°. Remove from oven and sprinkle chocolate chips and nuts on top. In small heavy pan, melt caramels in ⅓ cup evaporated milk; mix and pour over chips and nuts. Place remaining reserved cake mix on top. This may have to be done in dabs with a spoon as it will not spread easily. Bake for 15 to 20 minutes. Remove from oven and cool completely. Frost with 1 can milk-chocolate frosting. Cut in small squares.

APPLE CRISP

INGREDIENTS

8 to 10 apples, peeled and sliced
½ cup sugar
¾ cup flour
⅓ cup butter
1 teaspoon ground cinnamon

Place sliced apples in a casserole or other baking dish. Combine remaining ingredients and spread over apples. Bake at 325° until very slightly golden brown and crispy, about 30 to 45 minutes.

APPLE PIE

INGREDIENTS

2 (9-inch) frozen prepared pie pastry shells or
frozen pie pastry dough
8 to 10 apples, peeled, cored, and sliced
¾ cup sugar
2 tablespoons flour
½ teaspoon ground cinnamon
2 tablespoons butter, melted or cut into small pieces

Defrost pastry. Prepare apples. If using pastry dough, lightly flour underside of bottom pastry and place in pie pan. Shape by pressing pastry to bottom and sides of pan, allowing excess to fall over the outside rim of the pan. Prick bottom crust with fork. Fill shell with sliced apples. Sprinkle sugar, flour, and cinnamon on top. Drip melted butter or place butter pieces over all. Place second pie pastry on top and pinch rim edges to seal. Cut off excess dough. Pierce top with fork to allow steam to release. Place pan approximately 6 inches below upper heating unit. Bake at 400° until golden brown, approximately 40 to 50 minutes.

────────LAYERED CHOCOLATE──── PUDDING DESSERT

INGREDIENTS

1 cup chopped pecans
1 tablespoon butter
1½ sticks margarine
1 cup flour
8 ounces cream cheese
16 ounces whipped topping
1 cup powdered sugar
2 sliced bananas
3 small boxes dry instant chocolate
pudding or flavor of your choice
4 cups milk

Toast nuts: Place pecans in a pan with 2 teaspoons margarine. Mix. Heat in oven for 5 minutes at 350°. Remove from oven and set aside.

Layer I: Combine and mix together toasted nuts, flour, and margarine. Pat all on the bottom of a square 9" by 9" pan. Bake 30 minutes at 350°. Remove from oven and cool.

Layer II: In a medium-sized bowl, mix together cream cheese, powdered sugar, and 1 cup whipped topping. Place on top of cooled first layer.

Layer III: Top all with sliced bananas.

Layer IV: Mix dry pudding and milk together. Spread over bananas.

Layer V: Cover all with remaining whipped topping. Cover and refrigerate.

BANANA SPLIT CAKE

(no baking required)

INGREDIENTS

3 cups graham cracker crumbs
1 stick butter, melted
2 cups powdered sugar
2 sticks butter
2 whole eggs
1½ teaspoons vanilla
1 large can crushed pineapple, drained
1 large package frozen strawberries, thawed and drained
7 bananas, sliced and dipped in lemon juice
1 large container prepared whipped topping
½ cup chopped walnuts or pecans
12 maraschino cherries, cut in pieces

Layer I: Mix together graham cracker crumbs and 1 stick melted butter. Press in bottom of a 9" by 13" cake pan and chill for 45 minutes.

Layer II: Beat the following together for 20 minutes and spread on top of first layer: 2 sticks butter, powdered sugar, 2 eggs, and 1½ teaspoons vanilla.

Layer III: Add drained pineapple.

Layer IV: Add strawberries.

Layer V: Add bananas.

Layer VI: Add whipped topping and top all with nuts and cherries.

INGREDIENTS

1 cup butter
2 cups sugar
4 eggs
1 pint sour cream
2 teaspoons vanilla
4 cups flour
2 teaspoons baking powder
2 teaspoons baking soda

FOR FILLING:

½ cup brown sugar, packed
1 tablespoon flour
½ cup ground nuts

In large bowl, cream butter. Add sugar and mix. Add eggs, sour cream, vanilla, and mix. In separate bowl, sift flour, baking powder, and baking soda together and add to butter mixture. Set aside. In small bowl, combine brown sugar, flour, and nuts. Blend by hand. Grease and flour 2 loaf pans. Pour half of the butter batter into bottom of each pan. Reserve the other half of batter for top. Sprinkle half of the brown sugar-nut mixture over top. Pour remainder of butter batter over brown sugar-nut mixture. Top with reserved sugar-nut mixture. Bake in 350° preheated oven for 50 to 60 minutes. Test with toothpick.

SUGAR COOKIES

INGREDIENTS

1 cup butter
2 cups sugar
2 eggs
1 cup vegetable oil
pinch of salt
1 teaspoon vanilla
5 cups flour
2 teaspoons baking soda
2 teaspoons cream of tartar
1 cup sugar, on plate

With mixer, cream butter. Add sugar and mix well. Add next 4 ingredients and mix. In separate bowl, combine flour, baking soda, and cream of tartar. Add to cream mixture and mix. Roll dough into balls. Roll each ball onto a plate containing granulated sugar. Place balls on cookie sheet and flatten by pressing down on cookie with the bottom of a glass. Bake at 400° for approximately 10 minutes or until lightly browned on edges. Remove from baking tray and cool on paper towels.

QUICK FRUIT DESSERT

INGREDIENTS

1 (28 oz.) can chunk pineapple with syrup
1 (16 oz.) can apricots, juice drained
1 (16 oz.) can sliced peaches, juice drained
1 banana, sliced and coated with lemon juice
1 package instant dry lemon pudding

In large bowl, mix all of the above ingredients. Refrigerate. Any additional fresh fruit can be added. Cut fruit in large chunks. Serve in bowl or fruit cup or serve over plain pound cake.

CHEESECAKE SQUARES

INGREDIENTS

1 cup butter, softened
1 cup brown sugar, packed
1½ cups ground walnuts
3 cups flour
8 ounces cream cheese
¾ cup sugar
3 eggs
1½ teaspoons vanilla
4 tablespoons milk
1½ teaspoons lemon juice

Mix the first 4 ingredients. Reserve 3 cups. Spread and pack the remaining sugar-nut mixture in bottom of a greased and floured 10" by 14" cake pan. Bake at 350° for 12 minutes. While the above mixture is baking, combine the remaining ingredients together in a large bowl. Using an electric mixer, mix well and pour over the hot crust when it is removed from the oven. Sprinkle the remaining 3 cups of crumbs over the top of the cream mixture and return cake to oven. Bake approximately 25 to 30 minutes or until toothpick inserted into cake comes out clean. Remove from oven, cool, and cut into squares.

CHOCOLATE CHEESECAKE

INGREDIENTS

1 box German chocolate cake mix
4 eggs
1 stick melted butter
1 cup chopped walnuts
1 (8 oz.) package cream cheese
¾ cup powdered sugar

Set oven to 350°. Grease and flour a 9″ by 13″ cake pan. With mixer, combine cake mix, 2 eggs, and butter, mixing well. Add nuts and pour into cake pan. In another bowl, soften cream cheese, add 2 eggs and sugar. Mix all and pour over cake batter. Bake 25 to 30 minutes. Cheesecake is baked when toothpick inserted comes out clean and free of batter.

CHOCOLATE CHIPS

INGREDIENTS

2¼ cups sifted flour
1 teaspoon baking soda
1 teaspoon salt
1 cup (8 oz.) butter
¾ cup sugar
¾ cup brown sugar, packed
1 teaspoon vanilla
½ teaspoon water
2 eggs
1 (12 oz.) package chocolate chips, sweet or semi-sweet

In large bowl, combine and sift flour, soda, and salt. In second large bowl, mix all of the remaining ingredients, except the chocolate chips, with an electric mixer. Then add the sifted dry mixture and mix. Add chocolate chips. Mix by hand. Place spoonfuls of batter on cookie sheet or aluminum foil. Bake at 375° until lightly browned. Cool on absorbent paper towels.

——HALF MOONS OR BUTTER BALLS——

INGREDIENTS

1 pound butter
1 cup powdered sugar
4 cups flour
1 cup chopped or ground nuts

In large bowl, combine powdered sugar and flour. Mix well. In second large bowl, cream butter. Add flour mixture to butter. Add nuts and mix well with a spoon or spatula. Shape dough into small balls and/or crescents and bake on ungreased cookie tray until lightly browned, about 25 minutes. Remove from oven and cool on paper towels. When cool, sprinkle powdered sugar over the cookies with a sifter.

——————CHOCOLATE FUDGE——————

INGREDIENTS

3 cups sugar
¾ cup butter
⅔ cup evaporated milk
1 (12 oz.) package semi-sweet chocolate chips
1 (7 oz.) jar marshmallow cream
1 cup chopped nuts
1 teaspoon vanilla

In saucepan, combine sugar, butter, and milk. Bring to a slow boil, stirring constantly. Boil 5 minutes over medium heat, continuing to stir. Remove from heat. Add marshmallow cream, nuts, and vanilla. Beat all until blended. Pour into a buttered pan (about 9" by 13") and refrigerate. Cut into squares when cold.

Sauces, Gravies & Dips

─── MEAT SAUCE FOR SPAGHETTI ───

INGREDIENTS

2 tablespoons oil
1 pound ground beef
2 cloves garlic or ½ teaspoon garlic powder
½ teaspoon salt
¼ teaspoon pepper
½ teaspoon Italian seasoning
¼ teaspoon red pepper
1 whole onion *(optional)*
1 (28 oz.) can tomato sauce
Parmesan cheese, grated

On high heat, brown ground beef in heavy pot in hot oil. Lower heat and add garlic cloves or garlic powder. Add tomato sauce, Italian seasoning, red pepper, and whole onion. If thick, add some cold water. Stir, then cook covered, simmering for 30 minutes. Remove onion and garlic cloves. Serve over spaghetti, cooked according to package directions. Add grated Parmesan cheese. Prepared meatballs (see pp.22–23) can be added to the sauce.

─── MARINARA SAUCE ───

INGREDIENTS

1 (28 oz.) can crushed tomatoes
1 teaspoon garlic powder
½ teaspoon salt
¼ teaspoon pepper
¼ teaspoon red pepper flakes
½ teaspoon parsley flakes
1 teaspoon Italian seasoning
1 tablespoon Parmesan cheese, grated *(optional)*

Combine all of the above ingredients in a large skillet. Stir and simmer covered for 20 to 30 minutes. Add water if sauce gets too thick. Serve over any pasta. Top with additional grated Parmesan cheese.

BARBECUE SAUCE

INGREDIENTS

1 cup ketchup
2 tablespoons Worcestershire sauce
2 tablespoons vinegar
2 tablespoons sugar
½ teaspoon salt
dash of pepper

In heavy pot or skillet, combine and heat all of the above ingredients.

CHEESE SAUCE I

INGREDIENTS

1 pound processed cheese
½ cup milk

Heat milk and cheese in heavy saucepan over low heat. Stir until cheese is melted. Serve.

CHEESE SAUCE II

INGREDIENTS

1 cup warm milk
salt and pepper
2 tablespoons butter
8 to 10 slices American or Cheddar cheese
2 tablespoons cornstarch

In a heavy small pot, combine milk, salt, pepper, butter, and cheese and place over medium heat. Stir until creamy. Add cornstarch and mix. Serve.

QUICK GRAVY

INGREDIENTS

roast drippings (pork or beef)
2 heaping tablespoons flour
2 cups water
salt and pepper

Place roasting pan with drippings on stove burner and add water. Heat and scrape all drippings and hard crusts from sides of the pot and stir. Put 2 tablespoons flour in a cup and add very hot water a little at a time. Mix until slightly thickened and smooth. Add flour-water mixture to pot with drippings. Cook and stir. Add more water if gravy is too thick. Cook longer if gravy is too thin. Add salt and pepper if desired. Strain before serving.

COUNTRY GRAVY

INGREDIENTS

1 cup cold milk
2 tablespoons dry instant chicken gravy mix

Combine milk and gravy mix in small pan. Stir well. Heat to desired thickness while stirring to prevent gravy from sticking to pan. Add salt and pepper to taste.

INSTANT GRAVY

(dark or light)

INGREDIENTS

1 cup cold water
2 tablespoons instant chicken (for light) or brown (for dark) dry gravy mix

Combine water and gravy mix in small pan. Mix well. Heat and stir to dissolve mix until desired consistency is obtained. Add salt and pepper to taste.

DILL DIP

INGREDIENTS

1 pint sour cream
8 ounces cream cheese
2 tablespoons mayonnaise
1 small onion, grated
1½ tablespoons ground dill weed
pinch of Aunt Jan's crazy mixed-up salt *(optional)*

Combine all of the above ingredients and refrigerate.
Serve with raw vegetables.

SPINACH DIP

INGREDIENTS

1 package frozen spinach, thawed and drained
1 can bamboo shoots, drained
1 pint sour cream
1 cup mayonnaise
1 package dry vegetable soup mix
1 package dry onion soup mix

Mix all of the above ingredients together in a large
bowl and refrigerate. Serve with raw vegetables.

Microwave Cooking

ALL MICROWAVE OVENS do not cook at the same speed. Cooking time must be adjusted to suit your oven. Until you are familiar with your oven, check food being prepared frequently.

Microwave ovens are excellent for reheating leftovers. Do not use containers that are too small for the amount of food to be cooked to prevent spillovers. Use cooking utensils recommended in your manual. Never use metal utensils or aluminum foil.

Foods that take longer to cook should be placed on the outer rim of the container since food in the center will cook slower.

Pierce any food that is enclosed by a skin (i.e., potato or apple) to prevent the steam from splitting it open.

Paper towels, waxed paper, or plastic wrap can be used as a cover to prevent splashing.

NACHOS

INGREDIENTS

14 ounce bag of tortilla chips
8 ounce bag of shredded cheddar cheese
1 pound can of refried beans
1 small jar of stuffed green olives (sliced)
jalapeño peppers

Spread beans on each chip. Top with cheese. Add jalapeño peppers and olive slices. Arrange chips in a circle on paper plate. Heat on a moderately high level for 30 to 45 seconds, or until the cheese melts.

OATMEAL

INGREDIENTS

¼ cup oatmeal
½ cup water
½ cup milk
sugar to taste
dash of salt *(optional)*

Combine water and salt in container. Heat in microwave oven on full power for 1 minute. Add cereal and stir. Cook for 15 seconds. Serve with sugar and milk.

HOT CHOCOLATE

INGREDIENTS

¾ cup milk
1 tablespoon chocolate syrup
marshmallows *(optional)*

Place milk in cup, add syrup and stir. Heat for 1 to 1½ minutes. Top with marshmallows.

113

GRITS

INGREDIENTS

1 cup grits
5 cups water
1 tablespoon butter
¼ teaspoon salt
¼ teaspoon pepper

Combine grits and water in an 8-cup container and cook for 15 minutes on high power. Remove from oven and stir until smooth. Add salt, pepper, and butter.

BUTTERED RICE

INGREDIENTS

1 cup long grain rice
2½ cups cold water
1 teaspoon salt
1 tablespoon butter

Place all of the above ingredients in a 2 quart container. Cover and cook on high for 5 minutes. Stir and reduce heat to half power. Microwave for 20 minutes. Remove from oven and allow to stand 3 to 5 minutes. Can be served plain or with milk.

CANNED SOUP

INGREDIENTS

1 (10¾ oz.) can of condensed soup
1 can of water or milk (according to directions on can)

Place soup and liquid in container large enough to prevent boil over. Stir. Heat for 2 minutes. Stir. Heat additional 1 to 2 minutes.

BROCCOLI

INGREDIENTS

2½ pounds broccoli (washed, trimmed,
and cut into 4 to 5 inch lengths)
¼ cup water
4 tablespoons oil
½ teaspoon salt
1 lemon

Arrange broccoli in a circle with florets in the center
of cooking platter. Combine water and oil and pour
over broccoli. Add salt. Cook on high for 12 minutes.
Remove from oven and squeeze lemon juice over all.

BRUSSELS SPROUTS

INGREDIENTS

1 pound fresh brussels sprouts
¼ cup water
1 tablespoon butter *(optional)*
salt and pepper to taste

Cut off bottom end of stems. Wash in cold water. Make
a slit in bottom of each stem. Place sprouts in 1 quart
container with water. Cover and heat on high 8 to 9
minutes. Stir and allow to stand 1 to 2 minutes. Drain
and season with salt, pepper, and butter.

BREAD AND ROLLS

(to freshen)

To freshen bread or rolls wrap in paper towel. Heat 45
seconds to 1 minute. Bread must be eaten while still
warm; it will harden as it cools.

———MICROWAVE BAKED POTATO———

INGREDIENTS

potatoes
butter *(optional)*
sour cream *(optional)*
salt *(optional)*

Wash potatoes with cold water. Prick skins with fork. Microwave on paper towels according to time table below or until soft when pierced with a fork. Turn potatoes over halfway through cooking time. Remove from oven. Slit top of each potato in half. Serve with butter or sour cream.

1 potato—4 to 5 minutes

2 potatoes—6 to 7 minutes

3 potatoes—8 to 9 minutes

4 potatoes—10 to 11 minutes

6 potatoes—14 to 15 minutes

———GARLIC POTATOES———

INGREDIENTS

5 potatoes, scrubbed and pierced (cut in sections if desired)
3 large cloves of garlic, peeled and chopped
1½ tablespoons olive or vegetable oil
¼ tablespoon salt
dash of black pepper

Place potatoes in 1 quart container with sides. Add remaining ingredients and stir well coating potatoes. Place plastic wrap or lid on top of container to cover. Cook on high for approximately 9 to 11 minutes or until soft when pierced with a fork. Stir potatoes when halfway through cooking time.

─────STEAMED VEGETABLES─────

INGREDIENTS

vegetables of your choice (see examples below)
salt and pepper

The vegetables listed below can be steamed in the microwave. Place vegetables in a container and add 1 tablespoon of water or oil, salt and pepper to taste, and cover. If using plastic wrap, slit the top of the wrap or loosen one corner. Cook on full power according to the chart below. Times may vary according to make and size of microwave.

Broccoli	1½ pounds	10 to 11 minutes
Carrots	1 pound, sliced	6 to 8 minutes
Spinach	10 ounces	3 to 4 minutes
Zucchini	2 medium, sliced	4 to 6 minutes

─────ZUCCHINI 'N' SAUCE─────

INGREDIENTS

1 pound fresh zucchini, sliced
1 cup celery, sliced
½ teaspoon salt
⅛ teaspoon pepper
½ teaspoon garlic powder
¼ teaspoon Italian seasoning
1 (8 oz.) can tomato sauce
½ cup mozzarella cheese, shredded

Combine all ingredients except cheese and stir. Cover and cook on full power 8 to 10 minutes, or until vegetables are tender. Remove from microwave and sprinkle shredded cheese on top and return to oven. Cook 15 to 30 seconds until cheese is melted.

117

GLAZED CARROTS

INGREDIENTS

6 small carrots
1 tablespoon butter, cut in bits
1 tablespoon sugar

Place carrots in container. Scatter butter and sugar on top. Cover with plastic wrap and cook 7 minutes on high. Remove from oven and pierce plastic wrap. Allow to stand 1 to 2 minutes. Uncover and stir.

CORN-IN-HUSK

INGREDIENTS

5 ears of corn (quantity needed for
following cooking time)
butter
salt

Strip back husks, but leave attached to ear. Remove silk. Spread butter over corn and salt lightly. Replace husks and tie in place with string or rubber band. Arrange corn on oven glass tray. Cook on full power 4 minutes. Turn corn over and cook 4 to 5 minutes.

Note: For one ear of corn, cook 1½ to 2 minutes.

FISH FILLETS

INGREDIENTS

8 ounces flounder, cod, sole, or other choice
1 teaspoon butter *(optional)*
1 teaspoon lemon juice
garlic salt

Place fish on plate and season with remaining ingredients. Cover with paper towel. Microwave on high for 1 to 3 minutes, depending on thickness of fish.

MICROWAVED FISH

(1 serving)

INGREDIENTS

¼ pound fish fillet
½ tablespoon butter or margarine
1 teaspoon lemon juice
salt and pepper to taste

Arrange fish on glass serving plate. Dot with butter. Sprinkle with lemon juice. Season with salt and pepper. Cover with plastic wrap and poke a few holes in the wrap. Place in microwave oven on full power for 1 to 3 minutes or until fish flakes easily with fork. Remove excess liquid before serving.

MICROWAVED BACON

INGREDIENTS

2 to 12 slices of bacon

Arrange bacon on microwavable tray and cover with a paper towel, or arrange bacon on paper towel and cover with another paper towel. (Bacon may be layered with paper towels.) Cook until crisp.

APPROXIMATE COOKING TIME ON FULL POWER:

2 slices—1 minute 30 seconds to 2 minutes 20 seconds

4 slices—2 minutes 45 seconds to 4 minutes

12 slices—7 to 9 minutes

Note: Microwave should be wiped clean of any grease.

M
I
C
R
O
W
A
V
E

C
O
O
K
I
N
G

INGREDIENTS

4 apples, cored
¼ cup sugar
1 tablespoon butter
cinnamon

Remove circle of peel from top of each cored apple. Place apples on round glass container with sides. Add 1 tablespoon sugar to each cavity. Top with a small piece of butter and sprinkle each with cinnamon. Cover with plastic wrap. Cook on full power 3 to 4 minutes. Remove from oven and allow to cool for a few minutes.

Reference

SUGGESTED KITCHEN SUPPLIES

CASSEROLE OR SMALL ROASTING PAN
BAKING DISH
FRYING PAN OR SKILLET
TEA POT
BROILING PAN/*RACK
COFFEE MAKER
LARGE ENAMEL POT
MEDIUM-SIZED HEAVY POT
9-INCH PIE PLATE OR PAN
CUTTING KNIVES (1 LARGE AND 1 PARING KNIFE)
ELECTRIC HAND MIXER
CAKE PAN
COLANDER
2 MIXING BOWLS
CAN OPENER
WIRE WHISK
SPATULA
RUBBER TIP SPATULA
MEASURING SPOONS AND CUP
*SIFTER
SALT AND PEPPER SHAKERS
SUGAR BOWL
PLASTIC CONTAINERS FOR LEFTOVERS
*WOK
*MICROWAVE
FLATWARE
CANISTERS
DISHES
CUPS
GLASSES
GARBAGE CONTAINER
*FOOD CHOPPER/PROCESSOR

*Optional

WEIGHTS & MEASURES

3 teaspoons=1 tablespoon
4 tablespoons=¼ cup
16 tablespoons=1 cup
1 cup=½ pint
2 cups=1 pint
4 cups=1 quart
2 pints=1 quart
4 quarts=1 gallon
16 ounces=1 pound
1 cup shortening=½ pound
2 cups granulated sugar=1 pound
2¼ cups brown sugar, packed=1 pound
4 cups powdered sugar=1 pound
1 cup raw rice=4 cups cooked rice
9 graham crackers=1 cup crushed crackers

TIPS

Keep pad and pen handy for reminder notes, e.g., shopping lists, appointments, dates, meetings, etc.

Hang a calendar in a conspicuous place and note important long-term dates, e.g., birthdays, anniversaries, rent due, allergy shots, exams, medicine due, holidays, etc.

Save time when you need information; call on the phone rather than go.

While waiting for anything, get some little job out of the way or use the time for studying.

Discard junk mail and newspapers immediately. Put clothes away. Remove dirty clothing. Avoid clutter.

Start with good habits so they become automatic.

Start with fair rules to eliminate or prevent future arguments with roommates.

Save time in the morning by doing whatever you can the night before.

Collect an advance kitty to which all roommates contribute to pay for mutual expenses, e.g., toiletries, cooking spices, condiments, light bulbs, etc.

Cook more than you can eat. Freeze leftovers for a quick snack or future meal.

Use foil as a substitute container when baking pans are unavailable.

Use foil as a pot or pan liner whenever possible to eliminate hard clean-up jobs.

For vegetable dips, use French, round pumpernickel or rye breads as a container. Hollow out bread and remove the center. Wrap bread pieces. Freeze container and use cold.

There are many prepared quick-fix foods on the grocery shelves. Just follow package directions.

BASIC INGREDIENTS

SALT
PEPPER
SUGAR
GARLIC POWDER
PARSLEY FLAKES
CORNSTARCH
BAKING SODA
PAPRIKA
ITALIAN SEASONING
DRY MUSTARD
NUTMEG
RED PEPPER FLAKES
BROWN SUGAR
POWDERED SUGAR
CINNAMON SUGAR
OLIVES
WORCESTERSHIRE SAUCE
MAYONNAISE
KETCHUP
MUSTARD
VINEGAR
FLOUR
SHORTENING
VEGETABLE OIL
LIQUID SMOKE
TACO SEASONING
BREAD CRUMBS
OREGANO
MAPLE SYRUP
COCOA
HONEY
PICKLES
SOY SAUCE

INDEX OF RECIPES